THE DEEP

Unlocking the Hidden Supply of God Within You

Gerard Assey

THE DEEP:
Unlocking the Hidden Supply of God Within You

By

Gerard Assey

Published by:
Gerard Assey
19/18, Palli Arasan Street
Anna Nagar East
Chennai - 600 102

ISBN: 978-81-69340-16-8

Table of Contents

MASTER DECLARATION

I am sustained by the deep of God.
I will not run dry in any season.
There is a hidden supply beneath my life.
I will rise, stand, and flourish—
because God is my source.

PREFACE

There are seasons in life when everything around you appears dry.

Prayers feel unanswered. Doors seem closed. Efforts yield little visible result. In such moments, even sincere believers can begin to wonder: *"Where is the blessing of God in my life?"*

For many, the understanding of blessing has been limited to what is visible—open doors, financial increase, recognition, and favor that can be seen and celebrated. These are real, and they are good. Scripture speaks clearly of the "blessings of heaven above."

But there is another dimension—often overlooked, rarely taught, yet deeply powerful—the *blessings of the deep.*

This book was born out of that realization.

There is a supply that does not depend on circumstances.

There is a strength that does not fluctuate with seasons.

There is a reservoir beneath your life that does not run dry.

Whether you are in a season of abundance or in a place that feels like lack, this truth remains: God has not designed you to live only from what is happening around you, but from what He has already placed within and beneath you.

This is what makes this message different.

This is not just another teaching to inform your mind.

- ✓ It is identity-shifting — it will change how you see yourself. You will begin to recognize that you are not empty, not abandoned, and not at the mercy of circumstances. There is more within you than you have yet discovered.

- ✓ It is stability-giving — it will anchor you in uncertain seasons. When everything around you feels unstable, you will learn to draw from a deeper, unshakable source.
- ✓ It is faith-building — it will train your heart to trust what God is doing even when you cannot see it. You will begin to walk by conviction, not by visible evidence.

As you journey through these pages, my prayer is that this book will help you:

Stop panicking in dry seasons — because you will know that dryness around you does not mean emptiness within you.

Discover hidden strength — a strength that rises not from effort, but from divine supply.

Walk in quiet confidence — not loud, not boastful, but deeply assured that God is at work beneath the surface of your life.

Thrive when others struggle — not by comparison, but by connection to a source that does not fail.

You may not always see immediate change around you.

But something deeper will begin to happen *within* you.

- ✓ *Your perspective will shift.*
- ✓ *Your responses will change.*
- ✓ *Your confidence will grow—not in circumstances, but in God.*
- ✓ *And over time, what is hidden will begin to manifest.*

This is the way of the deep.

It is quiet.

It is unseen.

But it is powerful.
And once you learn to live from it, you will never again be at the mercy of external conditions.

- ✓ *You will live sustained.*
- ✓ *You will live steady.*
- ✓ *You will live from the deep.*

INTRODUCTION
More Than What You See

Opening Quote:

"What you see is not all there is. The greatest movements of God in your life often begin where your eyes cannot reach."

There are moments in a believer's life that are difficult to explain.

You are praying, yet nothing seems to move.

You are faithful, yet nothing appears to change.

You are standing, yet everything around you feels dry.

It is not a lack of faith.

It is not a lack of effort.

And often, it is not even a lack of blessing.

It is a lack of understanding.

Many of us have been taught to recognize the blessings that come from above—open doors, visible favor, financial increase, answered prayers that arrive quickly and clearly. These are real expressions of God's goodness. Scripture affirms them, and we rejoice in them.

In *Genesis 49:25*, when Jacob blesses Joseph, he speaks of *"blessings of heaven above."* These are the blessings we naturally celebrate. They are visible, measurable, and often immediate. They come like rain—refreshing, life-giving, and unmistakable.

But the same verse does not stop there.

It goes deeper. It speaks of *"blessings of the deep that lies beneath."*

This is where many believers lose clarity.

Because while the blessings from above are easy to recognize, the blessings from beneath are often hidden. They are not always visible. They do not always arrive with announcement or applause. Yet they are just as real—if not more essential.

If the blessings from above are like rain, then the blessings of the deep are like a well.

Rain falls from the sky. It is external, seasonal, and beyond your control. When it comes, the land rejoices. But when it delays, everything begins to dry.

A well, however, is different.

A well is not dependent on the season.

It is not affected by the absence of rain.

It draws from a source that is hidden beneath the surface.

You may not see it from the outside, but it is there—steady, quiet, and sustaining.

This is the life God intends for His people.

Not a life that survives only when conditions are favorable, but a life that is sustained even when conditions are not.

Yet many believers live as though rain is their only source.

When doors open, they rejoice.

When things go well, they feel blessed.

But when the season shifts—when prayers seem delayed, when opportunities dry up, when circumstances become difficult—they begin to feel as though something is wrong.

Questions arise quietly within the heart:

- ✓ *"Why is nothing happening?"*
- ✓ *"Have I done something wrong?"*
- ✓ *"Where is God in this season?"*

What is often missing in these moments is not God's presence, but God's perspective.

The truth is, you can be in a dry season externally and still be deeply supplied internally.
You can lack visible results and still carry unseen resources.
You can go through a season where nothing around you seems to respond, and yet something within you is being strengthened, developed, and sustained.
This is the mystery of the deep.

The prophet Isaiah records a powerful promise from God: *"I will give you the treasures of darkness and hidden riches of secret places"* (*Isaiah 45:3*). Notice the language—*treasures*, not in light, but in darkness; *riches*, not in open places, but in secret ones.
God does not limit His provision to what is visible.
Some of His greatest works happen in places where human eyes cannot see and human understanding cannot fully grasp.
We see this pattern throughout Scripture.
Joseph's life is one of the clearest illustrations. Before he ever stood in a palace, he was hidden in a pit. Before he interpreted dreams for kings, he sat in a prison where no one knew his name. From the outside, his life looked like a series of setbacks. But beneath the surface, something else was happening.
God was building depth.
There was a supply being formed within Joseph that no circumstance could take away. So when the famine came—not just to Egypt, but to the surrounding nations—Joseph did not collapse under pressure. He rose above it. While others were searching for survival, he had become a source.
That is the power of the deep.

In the New Testament, we see this again in the life of Jesus. For thirty years, there is silence. No miracles. No public ministry. No visible impact. To the natural observer, those years may seem insignificant. But they were not empty.

They were hidden.

And in that hiddenness, there was preparation. There was communion. There was alignment with the Father that would later sustain Him through opposition, rejection, and ultimately the cross.

When Jesus began His ministry, He did not operate from emptiness. He operated from fullness.

That fullness came from the deep.

Even today, this truth plays out in ways we often overlook.

Consider Ravi, a mid-level employee in a small firm. For years, he worked diligently, often unnoticed. Promotions passed him by. Others seemed to move ahead faster. There were moments when he questioned whether his efforts mattered.

Yet, instead of becoming bitter, he chose to grow quietly. He learned new skills. He strengthened his character. He deepened his faith.

Then, when an unexpected crisis hit the organization, leadership was shaken. Systems failed. Decisions needed clarity and stability. In that moment, Ravi was called upon—not because he had been the most visible, but because he had become the most dependable.

What had been built in the hidden seasons began to surface.

The deep began to speak.

Or take the story of Esther, a young woman navigating personal loss and uncertainty. After losing a close family member, she found herself in a season of emotional dryness. Prayers felt mechanical. Joy felt distant. Nothing outwardly seemed to change.

But instead of walking away, she stayed rooted.

She began journaling her thoughts. She meditated on Scripture, even when it felt difficult. Slowly, something began to shift—not around her, but within her.

Strength returned. Clarity emerged. Peace settled.

Months later, when a friend walked through a similar loss, Esther found herself able to comfort, guide, and strengthen her in ways she had never imagined. What she had received in the deep became a source for someone else.

This is what many fail to recognize.

God is not only working *for* you—He is working *in* you.

And often, the work within you is what prepares you for what will eventually come upon you.

If your life is built only on what is visible, then every change in circumstance will shake you.

But if your life is rooted in the deep, you become steady.

- ✓ *You learn to stand when others are shaken.*
- ✓ *You learn to trust when others are anxious.*
- ✓ *You learn to flow when others feel dry.*

This book is an invitation.

- ✓ *An invitation to shift your focus from what is seen to what is unseen.*
- ✓ *An invitation to discover that your life is not as empty as it may sometimes feel.*
- ✓ *An invitation to draw from a source that does not fail.*

There is more to your life than what you currently see.

There is a reservoir beneath you.
And once you learn to live from it, everything changes.

Declaration:
I refuse to judge my life by what is visible.
I believe that God is working beneath the surface.
Even when I do not see it, I am sustained by what He has placed within me.

CHAPTER 1:
SOURCE
When God Becomes Your Only Supply

Opening Quote:

"When every other source fails, you discover the One that never could."

There comes a point in every believer's life when what once felt stable begins to shift.

- ✓ *What you depended on starts to weaken.*
- ✓ *What you trusted begins to fail.*
- ✓ *What you assumed would always be there suddenly becomes uncertain.*

It is in such moments that a deeper question quietly rises within the heart:

What is truly my source?

For many, the honest answer is uncomfortable.

We say God is our source, but often, we draw our sense of security from something else—our job, our income, our relationships, our reputation, or even our own abilities. These things are not wrong in themselves, but they were never designed to carry the weight of being our source.

They are channels.

God alone is the source.

The psalmist writes in *Psalm 36:9*, "For with You is the fountain of life." Not a stream that runs dry. Not a supply that fluctuates. A fountain—constant, flowing, unending.

This is the first revelation of the deep: your life is sustained not by what surrounds you, but by what flows from God into you.
Jesus echoed this truth in a conversation that, at first glance, seemed ordinary. Sitting by a well, speaking to a Samaritan woman who had come simply to draw water, He said something that would redefine her understanding of supply:
"Whoever drinks the water I give them will never thirst. Indeed, the water I give them will become in them a spring of water welling up to eternal life" (*John 4:14*).
Notice the shift.
Not water given occasionally.
Not water stored externally.
But a spring placed *within*.
This is the life of the deep.
It is not dependent on access to external wells. It is not limited by seasons or circumstances. It flows from within because its origin is God Himself.
Yet, most believers do not start here.
We begin by trusting what we can see.
We feel secure when the salary is credited.
We feel confident when doors open.
We feel at peace when relationships are stable.
But what happens when these are shaken?
That is when God, in His wisdom, allows us to be brought into seasons where our external sources are reduced—not to harm us, but to redirect us.
This was the journey of Elijah.
In *1 Kings 17*, a severe drought had come upon the land. The natural systems that sustained life had failed. Rivers dried up. Crops withered. The very environment that people depended on had turned against them.

In the middle of this crisis, God speaks to Elijah and leads him to a brook called Cherith. There, something unusual happens. Ravens begin to bring him food—bread and meat, morning and evening.

It is an unexpected provision.

Not logical.

Not predictable.

Not explainable.

But deeply intentional.

God was teaching Elijah something that could not be learned in comfort—that his survival did not depend on the system around him, but on the God above him.

At Cherith, Elijah's source was not agriculture, not economy, not human support. It was God alone.

And yet, even that brook eventually dried up.

Why? Because God was not just providing for Elijah. He was preparing him.

When the brook dried, Elijah did not panic. He had already learned that his source was not the brook. So when God directed him again—this time to a widow in Zarephath—he obeyed.

And there, in another unlikely setting, provision continued.

The flour did not run out. The oil did not fail. The source remained the same. Only the channel changed.

This is where many struggle.

We become attached to the channel and forget the source.

- ✓ *When the job is stable, we begin to believe the job is the source.*
- ✓ *When relationships are strong, we begin to lean on them as our foundation.*

- ✓ *When things are going well, we subtly shift our dependence from God to what He has given.*

And when those things are shaken, we feel shaken too.

But the life of the deep calls us back. Back to a place where God alone is our supply.

Even Jesus lived from this reality. In *John 4:34*, He says, *"My food is to do the will of Him who sent Me and to finish His work."*

This is a profound statement.

Food sustains life. It gives energy, strength, and continuity. Yet Jesus was saying that His sustenance did not come merely from physical provision, but from alignment with the Father's will.

In other words, His source was not external—it was relational.

- ✓ *Even when He fasted for forty days, He was not empty.*
- ✓ *Even when He faced opposition, He was not shaken.*
- ✓ *Even when He stood alone, He was not abandoned.*

Because His life flowed from a deeper source.

This is what God desires for every believer—not independence from Him, but complete dependence on Him. Not a life where we occasionally turn to God in crisis, but a life where we consistently draw from Him as our source.

This truth becomes very real in everyday life, often in ways we do not expect.

Arun's story is one such example.

For over a decade, Arun ran a small but stable business. It was not extravagant, but it provided for his family. There was routine, predictability, and a sense of control.

Then, within a span of months, everything changed.

A combination of economic shifts and unforeseen losses caused his business to collapse. Clients withdrew. Payments were delayed. Eventually, he had to shut down operations completely.

The silence that followed was unsettling. For the first time in years, there was no steady income. No clear plan. No immediate solution.

At first, Arun did what most would do—he panicked.

He replayed decisions in his mind, questioned his choices, and feared for his family's future. But as the weeks passed, something began to shift—not outside, but within him.

With no business to manage, he found himself with time. Time he had never had before.

- ✓ *He began to pray—not out of routine, but out of need.*
- ✓ *He began to read Scripture—not for knowledge, but for strength.*
- ✓ *He began to listen—not for answers, but for direction.*

And slowly, small opportunities began to appear.

A friend asked him to help with a short-term project. It was modest, but it brought some income. Then another opportunity came—consulting for a small firm. Then a part-time assignment that used a skill he had almost forgotten he had.

None of these were large breakthroughs.

But together, they sustained him.

More importantly, they taught him something he had never fully understood before—that his life was not held together by his business, but by God.

Months later, when stability began to return, Arun found that something within him had changed.

He was less anxious. Less dependent on outcomes. More anchored.

The business he rebuilt was different—not just in structure, but in spirit. It was no longer his source. It was simply a channel.

That is the work of the deep.

God does not remove false sources to leave you empty. He removes them to reveal the true source.

Learning to live this way is not automatic. It requires intentional shifts.

It begins with honest reflection.

- ✓ *What do you turn to first when you feel uncertain?*
- ✓ *What gives you a sense of security?*
- ✓ *What, if taken away, would cause you to feel lost?*

These questions are not meant to condemn, but to reveal.

Because whatever you depend on most easily becomes your source.

But there is a better way.

A steadier way. A deeper way.

It is the way of daily dependence—not occasional, but consistent. A quiet, ongoing reliance on God, where you acknowledge Him not just in crisis, but in every part of your life.

It is the discipline of gratitude—even when things are not abundant. Not as denial, but as recognition that God is still present and still providing, even if the provision looks different.

It is the choice to trust—not in what you see, but in who God is.

Over time, something begins to change.

- ✓ *Fear loosens its grip.*
- ✓ *Anxiety loses its intensity.*
- ✓ *Confidence begins to rise—not in circumstances, but in God.*

And you begin to experience what Jesus spoke of—a spring, not outside you, but within you. *Flowing. Sustaining. Unfailing.*

At the end of it all, the question remains simple, yet deeply personal:

What am I truly depending on?

Your answer to that question will shape not only how you live, but how you stand when everything around you changes. Because when God becomes your only source, you discover something unshakable:

Even when channels fail… The source never does.

Declaration:

God is my source, not my circumstances.

I will not depend on what is around me, but on who is within me.

My supply is constant because my source is eternal.

CHAPTER 2:
SEED
What God Placed in You Before You Needed It

Opening Quote:

"Your future is not waiting to be given—it is already waiting within you."

There is a quiet mistake many believers make, often without realizing it.

We assume that when the demand comes, the supply must follow.

- ✓ *We pray for strength when the battle appears.*
- ✓ *We ask for wisdom when the decision arrives.*
- ✓ *We look for courage when the moment requires it.*

But God does not work that way.

He does not wait for the demand to arise before releasing the supply. He places the supply *within you* long before the moment ever comes.

This is the mystery of the seed.

A seed does not appear when the tree is needed. It is planted much earlier—hidden, unnoticed, often forgotten—until the right time comes for it to grow.

In the same way, God deposits capacity within you before life ever calls for it.

This is why *Ecclesiastes 3:11* says, *"He has made everything beautiful in its time. He has also set eternity in the human heart."*

There is something within you that is not accidental. There is a divine placement, a hidden potential, a quiet deposit that carries purpose.

The challenge is that seeds do not announce themselves.
They are not always visible. They do not always feel significant. And often, they remain dormant until something—usually pressure, responsibility, or crisis—awakens them.
Many people spend years looking outward for what God has already placed inward.
They compare, they strive, they imitate others, not realizing that their provision is already within them, waiting to be recognized and developed.

This truth is beautifully illustrated in the life of Joseph.
Long before Joseph ever stood before Pharaoh, long before he managed the resources of a nation, he had a dream. In fact, he had two. These dreams were not just symbolic; they were seeds.
They carried within them the blueprint of his future.
At the time, Joseph did not fully understand them. Others misunderstood them even more. His brothers rejected him. His circumstances contradicted what he had seen. Instead of rising, he was thrown into a pit. Instead of being honored, he was sold. Instead of leading, he served. Instead of being free, he was imprisoned.
If Joseph had measured his life only by his circumstances, he would have concluded that nothing in him was working.
But the seed was still there.
The dream did not disappear in the pit.
It was not erased in slavery.
It was not destroyed in prison.
It remained. Quiet. Hidden. Alive.

And when the time came—when Pharaoh needed interpretation, when Egypt needed leadership, when the world faced famine—the seed that had been planted years earlier began to manifest.

Joseph did not suddenly become capable. He revealed what had already been deposited. That is how God works.

He places within you what your future will require, even when your present does not seem to need it.

We see the same principle in the New Testament through the life of Timothy.

Timothy was not a loud or dominant personality. By all accounts, he seemed reserved, perhaps even hesitant. Yet Paul saw something in him that Timothy himself may not have fully recognized.

In *2 Timothy 1:6*, Paul writes, *"Fan into flame the gift of God, which is in you…"*

Notice the wording—*which is in you.* Not something you will receive. Not something you must go searching for. But something already present.

The instruction was not to acquire a gift, but to stir it.

- ✓ *To awaken it.*
- ✓ *To develop it.*
- ✓ *To allow it to grow into its full expression.*

Timothy's effectiveness in ministry did not come from imitation. It came from activation.

What was within him had to be recognized, nurtured, and brought to life.

Paul reinforces this truth again in *2 Corinthians 9:10*: *"Now He who supplies seed to the sower… will also supply and increase your store of seed…"*

God is both the giver and the multiplier of seed. But He does not multiply what is not sown, and He does not activate what is not acknowledged.

This is where many remain stuck. Not because they lack potential, but because they overlook what they already carry.
Life, however, has a way of uncovering what is hidden. Often, it is not comfort that reveals your capacity—it is pressure.

Meera's story reflects this in a very real way.
For years, Meera worked as a schoolteacher in a mid-sized institution. She was consistent, dependable, and sincere in her work. She did not seek attention, nor did she see herself as a leader. She simply did what was required, day after day.
If someone had asked her about her strengths, she would have mentioned patience, maybe diligence—but leadership would not have made the list.
Then, unexpectedly, the school entered a season of disruption.
The principal resigned abruptly. Administrative confusion followed. Teachers were uncertain, students were unsettled, and parents began to raise concerns. In the absence of clear leadership, the environment began to drift.
During those days, something began to shift within Meera.
It did not happen dramatically. There was no sudden announcement or visible transformation. But she began to take small steps.
She started organizing informal meetings among teachers.
She created simple plans to bring structure to the day.
She took initiative in communicating with parents.
She stepped into situations she would have previously avoided.

At first, she questioned herself. *"Am I overstepping? Am I capable of this?"*

But the more she stepped forward, the more clarity she found.

Others began to respond. Teachers began to rely on her. Students felt stability. Parents expressed confidence. What had been hidden began to emerge.

Months later, when the school board formally appointed her to a leadership role, many saw it as a natural progression. But for Meera, it was a revelation.

She had not become someone new.

She had discovered what had always been there.

The seed had been planted long before the crisis. The crisis simply revealed it.

This is how God often works in our lives. He places gifts, abilities, perspectives, and capacities within us, not always for immediate use, but for future expression.

The problem is not that we lack seed. The problem is that we often look elsewhere.

- ✓ *We compare our beginnings with someone else's maturity.*
- ✓ *We measure our quiet seasons against someone else's visible success.*
- ✓ *We underestimate what is within us because it does not yet look like what we expect.*

But seeds do not look like trees. They do not resemble the fullness of what they will become. They carry it. And if they are nurtured, protected, and given time, they will grow.

Learning to live from the deep means learning to value what God has already placed within you. It requires a shift in attention—from comparison to recognition.

You begin to notice patterns in your life.

- ✓ *Things that come naturally to you.*
- ✓ *Burden areas that stir your heart.*
- ✓ *Moments where you feel unexpectedly alive or effective.*

These are not random. They are indicators of seed. It also requires patience.

Seeds do not grow overnight. They require cultivation. Time. Consistency. There are seasons where nothing seems to be happening, yet beneath the surface, roots are forming.

And perhaps most importantly, it requires responsibility. What is within you must be developed.

Not neglected.

Not ignored.

Not postponed.

But stewarded. Because what God has placed within you is not only for you. It is meant to serve others, to meet needs, to bring life where there is lack.

As you grow in this understanding, something begins to change.

You stop searching frantically for what you think you lack. You begin to explore faithfully what you already have. You become less distracted by others' journeys and more committed to your own.

And slowly, quietly, steadily, the seed begins to grow.

Until one day, what was once hidden becomes visible. What was once small becomes significant. What was once unnoticed becomes undeniable.

And you realize that God, in His wisdom, had already provided what you needed—long before you knew you would need it.

So the question is not whether you have been given anything.

The question is:

What has God already placed inside you?
And are you willing to recognize it, nurture it, and allow it to grow? Because within you, even now, there is seed. And within that seed… is your future.

Declaration:
I carry divine potential within me.
What I need for my future, God has already placed inside me.
I will recognize, nurture, and release what He has deposited in my life

CHAPTER 3:
SECRET
The Power of What God Hides

Opening Quote:

"God does His deepest work in places where no one is watching and nothing is announced."

There is something deeply unsettling about seasons where nothing seems to be happening.

You are praying, but there is no visible answer.

You are working, but there is no recognition.

You are believing, but there is no evidence.

To the natural mind, these seasons feel like delay.

To the human heart, they often feel like neglect.

But in the economy of God, hidden does not mean absent. silence does not mean inactivity. In fact, some of God's most profound work happens in places where nothing is seen and nothing is announced.

This is the power of the secret.

Deuteronomy 29:29 says, *"The secret things belong to the Lord our God…"* There are dimensions of God's working that are not immediately visible, not instantly understandable, and not publicly displayed. They belong to Him—not because He is withholding from us, but because He is *preparing something within us.*

Jesus reinforces this in *Matthew 6:6* when He says, *"When you pray, go into your room, close the door and pray to your Father, who is unseen. Then your Father, who sees what is done in secret, will reward you."*

Notice the pattern.
There is a secret place.
There is a hidden process. And there is a revealed reward.
But the order matters.
God does not begin with public display. He begins with private formation.
This is where many struggle.
We want the visible without embracing the invisible.
We desire manifestation without submission to preparation.
We long for recognition without being willing to be hidden.
Yet, the life of the deep cannot be built in the open alone. It must be formed in the secret.

Few lives illustrate this better than Joseph's.
Joseph's story is often celebrated for its ending—standing in authority, managing a nation, saving generations from famine. But that visible moment was built upon years of hidden process.
Before the palace, there was a prison.
And the prison was not just a place of confinement—it was a place of concealment.
Joseph was not just physically hidden; he was forgotten. Even those he helped failed to remember him. Days turned into months. Months stretched into years. No announcement. No indication that anything was about to change.
From the outside, it looked like nothing was happening.
But in the secret, everything was happening.

- ✓ *Character was being formed.*
- ✓ *Patience was being refined.*
- ✓ *Discernment was being sharpened.*

Joseph was not wasting time. He was being prepared.
So when the moment came—when Pharaoh needed interpretation, when Egypt needed leadership—Joseph did not rise as a man suddenly gifted. He emerged as a man already prepared.
The secret had done its work.
The same pattern is seen, even more profoundly, in the life of Jesus.
We often focus on His ministry—the miracles, the teachings, the crowds. But those three years of public ministry were preceded by thirty years of hidden life.
Thirty years.
No public platform.
No recorded miracles.
No visible influence.
Just quiet obedience. Daily submission. Unseen growth.
To the natural observer, those years might seem uneventful. But they were essential.
Because when Jesus stepped into His public calling, He carried a depth that could not have been manufactured in the spotlight. It had been cultivated in the secret.

- ✓ *When opposition came, He was not shaken.*
- ✓ *When crowds gathered, He was not distracted.*
- ✓ *When pressure increased, He remained anchored.*

Why? Because His life had roots in the unseen.
This is where many believers misinterpret their journey. They measure progress only by visibility.

- ✓ *If something is seen, it is valued.*
  If something is recognized, it is affirmed.

If something is celebrated, it is considered successful.

But God measures differently.
He values what is formed in the hidden.
He honors what is done without applause.
He builds in secret what He intends to reveal in time.
This truth becomes very real in everyday life, often in ways that are easy to overlook.

Daniel Raj's story is one of quiet faithfulness.
For nearly twelve years, Daniel worked in a mid-level role within a large organization. He was consistent, disciplined, and deeply committed to his work. Yet, year after year, promotions passed him by.
Others who were louder, more visible, or better connected seemed to move ahead. Daniel remained where he was.
There were moments when he questioned himself. *"Am I missing something? Is this where I will always be?"*
But instead of becoming bitter, he chose a different path.
He continued to improve his skills.
He took on responsibilities that others avoided.
He learned to lead, even without a title.
He chose integrity, even when it cost him recognition.
Most of this went unnoticed. There were no announcements. No awards. No sudden breakthroughs.
Just quiet, consistent growth. Then, one year, everything shifted.
A major restructuring took place within the organization. Leadership positions opened unexpectedly. Decisions had to be made quickly. In

that moment, those who had been highly visible were not necessarily the most reliable.

Daniel's name surfaced—not because he had demanded attention, but because over time, he had earned trust.

Within a short span, he was elevated into a leadership role that far exceeded anything he had previously held.

To many, it looked sudden.

But it was not sudden. It was revealed.

Years of hidden preparation had surfaced in a single moment.

This is how God often works. He does not rush the process to satisfy our desire for visibility. He completes the process to ensure our readiness for responsibility.

The difficulty, of course, is learning to trust Him in the hidden.

Hidden seasons test something very deep within us.

They test our motives.

They test our patience.

They test our identity.

- ✓ *Will you remain faithful when no one sees?*
- ✓ *Will you continue to give your best when there is no recognition?*
- ✓ *Will you trust God when there is no visible evidence that anything is changing?*

These are not easy questions. Because the human heart longs for affirmation. It longs to know that what it is doing matters.

But in the secret, affirmation often comes from God alone. And that is where true depth is formed. Learning to embrace hidden seasons is not about pretending they are easy. It is about recognizing their

purpose. You begin to see that obscurity is not rejection—it is protection.
God hides what He values until it is ready.

- ✓ *A seed is hidden in the ground before it becomes a tree.*
- ✓ *A foundation is buried before a building is raised.*

Roots grow downward before branches extend outward.
Hiddenness is not a delay of purpose. It is the development of it. Faithfulness in obscurity then becomes a choice.
A daily decision to show up. To give your best. To remain consistent.
Not because others are watching, but because God is. And in doing so, something begins to shift within you.
You become less dependent on external validation. Less driven by recognition. More anchored in purpose.
Finally, there is the matter of timing. Perhaps one of the most difficult aspects of hidden seasons is not knowing *when* things will change.
We often want clarity. A timeline. A sign that breakthrough is near. But God rarely works according to our schedules. He works according to readiness.
Joseph was released when the moment required him. Jesus stepped forward when the time was fulfilled. Daniel Raj was elevated when the organization needed what he carried.
Not before. Not after. But at the right time.
Trusting divine timing means letting go of the need to control the process.

It means believing that God sees what you are doing, even when others do not.
It means holding onto the quiet assurance that nothing invested in the secret is ever wasted.
And perhaps that is where this chapter settles—not in a dramatic conclusion, but in a quiet, honest question:

- ✓ *Can I trust God when nothing is visible?*
- ✓ *Can I trust Him when there is no applause?*
- ✓ *When there is no recognition?*
- ✓ *When there is no immediate result?*

Because if you can trust Him there— in the unseen in the hidden, in the secret— then when the time of revelation comes, you will not just step into visibility. You will step into it with depth. And that depth will sustain you long after the moment has passed.

Declaration:
I will trust God in hidden seasons.
What is unseen in my life is not wasted—it is being prepared.
In due time, what God is forming in secret will be revealed.

CHAPTER 4:
STRENGTH
Drawing from the Deep When Life Drains You

Opening Quote:

"When life takes from you, God draws from within you."

There are seasons in life that do not just challenge you—they drain you.

Not loudly. Not all at once. But slowly, steadily, almost quietly.

You wake up tired, even after rest. You find yourself thinking more, but feeling less. You continue to function, but something within you feels reduced.

It is not always visible to others. In fact, from the outside, everything may appear normal. Responsibilities are met. Conversations are carried. Life moves on.

But inside, there is a quiet depletion.

These are the moments that reveal where your strength truly comes from.

Because when life is full and everything is working, strength is easy to assume. But when life begins to drain you—through pressure, disappointment, loss, or prolonged uncertainty—you discover very quickly whether your strength is external or internal.

- ✓ *If your strength is drawn from circumstances, it will rise and fall with them.*
- ✓ *If your strength is drawn from people, it will fluctuate with their presence and support.*

- ✓ *But if your strength comes from the deep, it will remain—even when everything else feels unstable.*

This is the kind of strength God offers. Not temporary relief, but sustained inner capacity. The prophet writes in *Isaiah 12:3*, *"With joy you will draw water from the wells of salvation."*

Notice the language. Strength is not handed to you passively. It is drawn.

There is a well. There is a source. But there is also participation. You must learn how to draw from it.

Paul echoes this truth in *Ephesians 3:16*, where he prays that believers would be *"strengthened with power through His Spirit in your inner being."*

Not just outwardly. Not just situationally. But inwardly.

This is the strength of the deep—a strength that forms within you and sustains you when everything around you feels uncertain.

We see this lived out powerfully in the life of David.

In *1 Samuel 30*, David returns to Ziklag only to find devastation. The city has been burned. Their families have been taken captive. Everything they held dear is gone.

It is not just loss—it is overwhelming loss.

And then, as if that were not enough, the people who stood with him begin to turn against him. The same men who followed him now speak of stoning him.

In one moment, David loses his home, his family, and the support of those closest to him. If there was ever a moment to collapse, this was it.

But the Scripture records something remarkable: *"David strengthened himself in the Lord his God."*

There is no indication that circumstances changed immediately. The loss was still real. The pain was still present. The threat was still near. But David turned inward—toward God.

- ✓ *He did not wait for someone to encourage him.*
- ✓ *He did not depend on external reassurance.*
- ✓ *He drew strength from the deep.*

That act did not erase his situation, but it transformed his response to it.

And from that place of regained strength, he was able to seek direction, pursue what was lost, and recover all. The victory began not in the battle, but in the strengthening.

In the New Testament, we see a similar depth of strength in the life of Paul.

Paul's journey was not easy. It was marked by hardship, opposition, and suffering. Yet one of the most powerful glimpses of his inner life comes from a place where most would expect weakness—prison.

In *Philippians 4:13*, Paul writes, *"I can do all things through Christ who strengthens me."*

These are not words written in comfort. They come from confinement.

He is restricted, uncertain of his future, and physically limited. Yet, there is no sense of defeat in his words.

Why? Because his strength was not tied to his situation. It was rooted in Christ.

Even in prison, he writes with clarity, with conviction, and even with joy. His environment could not dictate his inner condition.

That is the strength of the deep.

It does not deny the reality of difficulty. It transcends it. It allows you to feel the weight of life without being crushed by it. In everyday life, this kind of strength often emerges in the most human and relatable ways.

Lydia's story is one such example.
Lydia was known among her friends as warm, dependable, and quietly strong. She had built a simple but meaningful life, centered around her family and her work.
Then, without warning, loss entered her life.
The sudden passing of someone deeply close to her left a space that could not be easily filled. The days that followed were heavy. Routine became difficult. Even simple tasks required effort.
There were moments when she felt completely empty.
Not physically exhausted, but emotionally drained. Not outwardly broken, but inwardly unsettled. At first, she tried to manage it by staying busy. Filling her time. Avoiding stillness. But the emptiness remained. Then, slowly, she began to return to something she had always known, but never needed this deeply before.
She began to sit quietly in God's presence.
There were no elaborate prayers. Sometimes, no words at all. Just stillness. Just honesty. Just presence.
She began to read small portions of Scripture—not to study, but to steady herself.
She began to speak simple truths over her life—even when she did not feel them.
She allowed herself to grieve, but not without hope.
It was not immediate.
There were days when the heaviness remained. There were moments when the questions returned.

But over time, something began to shift. Strength began to rise—not dramatically, but steadily.
She found herself able to face the day again. To engage with others again. To carry what she once thought she could not. Months later, something unexpected happened.
A colleague of hers went through a similar loss. In those early days of confusion and pain, Lydia found herself stepping in—not with perfect answers, but with quiet strength.
She listened. She supported. She encouraged.
And in doing so, she realized something. The strength she had received in her own season of emptiness had not only sustained her—it had prepared her to sustain someone else.
This is the nature of strength that comes from the deep.
It is not loud.
It is not always visible.
But it is real. And it grows in places where you learn to draw from God, not occasionally, but consistently.

Learning to draw from this strength is a process.
It begins with building rhythms that connect you to God—not out of obligation, but out of need. Moments in your day where you pause, reflect, and realign. Not because everything is falling apart, but so that when it does, you are already rooted.
It grows as you learn to speak life—not just over situations, but over yourself. Words shape perspective, and perspective influences strength. What you repeatedly tell yourself matters more than you may realize.
It deepens as you develop emotional resilience—the ability to feel fully without losing stability. To

acknowledge pain without surrendering to it. To process honestly without becoming overwhelmed.

These are not instant changes. They are formed over time. And as they are formed, something remarkable begins to happen.

You become less reactive. Less easily shaken. More grounded.

You still face challenges.

You still experience loss.

You still have moments of weakness.

But you are no longer defined by them. Because beneath it all, there is strength.

Not borrowed. Not temporary. But deeply rooted. And so, the question becomes personal. Not theoretical, but real.

- ✓ *Where do I go when I feel empty?*
- ✓ *Do I turn to distraction?*
- ✓ *To people?*
- ✓ *To temporary relief?*

Or do I learn to draw from the well that never runs dry?

Because when you learn to draw from that well—when you begin to access the strength that God has placed within your reach— you discover something powerful:

Life may drain you at times… But it does not have the power to empty you.

Not when your strength comes from the deep.

Declaration:

My strength is not dependent on my situation.

I am strengthened in my inner being by the Spirit of God.

Even when I feel empty, I am sustained by a deeper supply.

CHAPTER 5:
SEPARATION
Why the Deep Sets You Apart

Opening Quote:
"You do not stand out by striving above others, but by being rooted deeper than them."

There is a question that quietly shapes the direction of every life:
What makes me different?
Not different in appearance, not different in personality—but different in substance. Different in how you respond, how you endure, how you rise when others fall.
Most people seek distinction through visibility. They try to stand out by doing more, achieving more, or being seen more. But the distinction that lasts—the kind that remains through seasons of pressure, uncertainty, and change—does not come from what is on the surface.
It comes from depth. Depth is what separates.
It is not always obvious at first. In fact, in calm seasons, people can appear very similar. When everything is stable, when opportunities are abundant, when conditions are favorable, the differences between lives are not always clear.
But when the season shifts—when pressure increases, when resources tighten, when uncertainty rises—that is when distinction begins to show.
Because depth responds differently.
This is the essence of what Moses speaks over Joseph in *Deuteronomy 33:13*: *"Blessed of the Lord*

be his land, with the precious things of heaven above, and with the deep that lies beneath."

There are blessings that come from above—visible, shared, and often experienced by many. But the blessing of the deep is what sets a person apart.

It is not seasonal. It is not dependent on environment. It is not easily shaken.

It gives a person the ability to thrive where others struggle.

We see this clearly in the life of Isaac.

In *Genesis 26:1*, the land was gripped by famine. Resources were scarce. The natural instinct in such a time is to retreat, to relocate, to look for better conditions elsewhere. Isaac himself considered going to Egypt, a place known for stability in times of crisis.

But God gave him a different instruction: to remain where he was.

This was not logical.

Why stay in a land that could not sustain itself? Why remain in a place where others were leaving?

Yet Isaac obeyed.

And then something remarkable happened.

"In that land he sowed and reaped in the same year a hundredfold; and the Lord blessed him" (*Genesis 26:12*).

This is not just prosperity—it is distinction.

Others were experiencing lack. Isaac experienced abundance.

Others were reacting to the environment. Isaac was responding to God.

The difference was not the land. It was the depth.

Isaac's life was not governed by external conditions. It was anchored in something deeper—his relationship with God, his obedience, his trust. And because of that, he operated differently.

Even when conflict arose—when wells were contested and taken—Isaac did not react with fear or desperation. He moved, dug again, and continued.
Why? Because he understood something.
If the source is beneath you, you are not limited by what is around you.
You can dig again.
You can build again.
You can rise again.
This is the kind of life that stands out—not because it demands attention, but because it carries substance.

We see a similar pattern in the New Testament, in the early church.
After the resurrection of Jesus, the believers began to grow in number and influence. But growth was soon met with resistance. Persecution arose. Opposition intensified. Believers were scattered. From a natural perspective, this should have weakened the movement. But it did not. It strengthened it.
In *Acts 8:4*, we read, *"Those who had been scattered preached the word wherever they went."*

- ✓ *They did not retreat.*
- ✓ *They did not collapse.*
- ✓ *They did not lose their identity.*

Instead, they carried what was within them into every place they went.
Their faith was not dependent on comfort. Their conviction was not tied to safety. Their strength was not based on circumstances. They had depth.
And that depth created distinction.
While others might have withdrawn under pressure, they expanded. While opposition tried to contain

them, it actually caused them to spread. This is the paradox of the deep.

What is meant to reduce you can reveal you.

What is meant to stop you can distinguish you.

Because when your life is rooted in God, external pressure does not diminish you—it defines you.

This truth continues to unfold in everyday life, often in ways that are both subtle and powerful.

Vikram's story reflects this in a very practical way.

For years, Vikram worked steadily in the manufacturing sector. His growth was gradual, his progress consistent but not extraordinary. He was disciplined, thoughtful, and quietly committed to doing things well.

Then came a significant economic downturn. Orders reduced. Costs increased. Companies began to cut back. Many around him—colleagues, competitors, even well-established businesses—began to struggle. Some shut down. Others scaled back drastically.

Fear became common. Conversations shifted from growth to survival.

In the middle of this environment, Vikram faced the same pressures as everyone else. There were real challenges. Decisions had to be made. Risks had to be managed.

But something about his response was different.

He did not rush into panic. He did not make reactive decisions. He did not follow the crowd. Instead, he slowed down.

He revisited his processes. He strengthened relationships with clients.

He explored smaller, consistent opportunities rather than chasing uncertain large ones.
He remained steady when others became unstable.
At the same time, his personal discipline deepened. He spent time in reflection, in prayer, in aligning his decisions with a sense of purpose rather than pressure.
It was not dramatic.
There were no sudden breakthroughs. But over time, something began to shift.
While others continued to struggle, Vikram's business stabilized. Then, gradually, it began to grow. Opportunities opened—not because the environment had improved, but because his approach had remained anchored.
Years later, when the market recovered, Vikram was not just surviving—he was positioned. What had set him apart was not luck. It was not timing. It was depth. He had learned to operate from within, not just react to what was happening around him.
This is what the deep produces.
It creates a kind of life that is not easily shaken by trends, not easily influenced by pressure, not easily defined by circumstances. But this kind of depth does not happen accidentally. It requires choices.
There is a decision not to follow the crowd, especially when the crowd is driven by fear or urgency. It is not always easy to take a different path, particularly when others seem to be moving faster or more visibly. But depth often requires you to move differently.
There is also a commitment to develop your inner life. To grow spiritually. To remain connected to God, not just in need, but in consistency. Because what

sustains you in pressure is not what you build in the moment—it is what you have built over time.

And above all, there is a choice to remain rooted.

- ✓ *Rooted in truth.*
- ✓ *Rooted in faith.*
- ✓ *Rooted in God.*

Roots are not visible. They do not attract attention. But they determine stability.

When storms come—and they will—it is not the height of the tree that determines whether it stands. It is the depth of its roots.

And so, distinction is not something you chase. It is something that emerges.

Quietly.

Steadily.

Naturally.

As you grow deeper, you become different. Not because you are trying to stand out, but because you are standing on something others are not.

And this leads us back to a question that is both simple and searching:

- ✓ *What makes my life different?*
- ✓ *Is it what I have?*
- ✓ *Is it what I achieve?*
- ✓ *Is it what others see?*

Or is it something deeper—something rooted, something steady, something that remains even when everything else changes?

Because when your life is built on the deep, you will not just survive difficult seasons.

You will stand out in them. And that distinction will not only sustain you—it will point others to the source beneath your life.

Declaration:
I am set apart by the depth God has built within me. I will not be shaped by the environment—I will rise above it.
In every season, I will flourish because my roots run deep.

FINAL CHAPTER:
THE FLOW
Living Daily from the Deep

Opening Quote:

"The deep was never meant to stop with you—it was meant to flow through you."

There is a difference between visiting a truth and living from it.
You can hear about the deep and be inspired.
You can understand its principles and even agree with them.
But the true transformation happens when the deep is no longer a concept you admire—but a reality you live from. Because the goal is not simply to know that there is a source beneath you.
The goal is to live from it—daily, consistently, quietly.
To wake up each day not dependent on what may or may not happen around you, but anchored in what is already flowing within you.
This is the life of the flow.
Jesus described it in a way that shifts everything.
In *John 7:38*, He said, *"Whoever believes in Me, as Scripture has said, rivers of living water will flow from within them."*
Notice the language carefully.
Not a cup. Not a limited portion. Not something you visit occasionally.

- ✓ *Rivers.*
- ✓ *Continuous.*
- ✓ *Moving.*
- ✓ *Overflowing.*

And not flowing *to* you—but flowing *from* you.
This is the final expression of the deep.
At first, you discover the source.
Then you recognize the seed.
You learn to trust the secret.
You draw strength from within.
You begin to live with distinction.
But it does not end there. It leads to something greater.
You become a channel. A carrier. A supplier.
This is where the journey matures. Because in the beginning, much of your walk with God is about survival. Learning to trust Him. Learning to depend on Him. Learning to find strength in Him.
But as you grow, something shifts.
You are no longer just drawing for yourself. You begin to carry for others. The deep within you begins to flow outward.

We see glimpses of this even in the Old Testament.
Consider the life of Joseph again, but now from a different perspective.
In the early stages, Joseph was sustained by what God had placed within him. The dream carried him through the pit, through slavery, through prison.
But when he stepped into his position in Egypt, something changed.
He was no longer just surviving. He was supplying.
During the famine, nations came to Egypt—not because Egypt was naturally abundant, but because Joseph had stewarded what God had revealed to him.
What had once sustained Joseph now sustained others.
The deep had become a flow.

In the New Testament, this principle is seen powerfully in the early church.
After receiving the Holy Spirit, the believers did not gather to protect what they had received. They moved outward.

- ✓ *They taught.*
- ✓ *They served.*
- ✓ *They gave.*
- ✓ *They encouraged.*

In *Acts 4:33*, it says, *"With great power the apostles continued to testify… and God's grace was so powerfully at work in them all."*
And then something remarkable follows—there were no needy persons among them.
Why? Because those who had began to give.
Those who were strengthened began to strengthen others.
Those who had received began to release.
This is the flow.

- ✓ *It is not forced.*
- ✓ *It is not artificial.*
- ✓ *It is the natural outcome of a life rooted in the deep.*

The river within you does not exist only for you. It exists to flow through you.
This truth becomes deeply personal when it begins to take shape in everyday life.

Samuel's story reflects this in a simple yet powerful way.
Samuel worked in a demanding corporate environment. The pace was relentless, the expectations high, and the pressure constant. For

years, he struggled to keep up—not just with the workload, but with the emotional weight of it.

There were seasons when he felt overwhelmed, stretched thin, and quietly exhausted.

It was during one such season that he began to take his inner life more seriously.

Not out of routine, but out of necessity.

He carved out small moments in his day to pause, reflect, and reconnect with God. Not long hours, but consistent ones. He began to read Scripture not for information, but for alignment. He learned to be still, even in the middle of activity.

Over time, something changed. The external demands did not reduce. But his internal response shifted.

He became calmer. More focused. Less reactive.

Situations that once overwhelmed him began to feel manageable.

But the real shift came when others began to notice.

Colleagues who were struggling with stress started approaching him—not because he had all the answers, but because he carried a certain steadiness.

He listened. He encouraged. He shared simple insights that had helped him.

Without planning it, Samuel became a source.

What had once been his personal survival had become someone else's support.

This is how the deep flows. Not always through platforms or positions, but through presence.

Through how you respond. Through how you speak. Through how you carry others.

Living from the deep daily is not about dramatic experiences.

- ✓ *It is about consistent connection.*

- ✓ *It is about waking up with an awareness that your life is not dependent on what you will face, but on who is within you.*
- ✓ *It is about returning, again and again, to that inner place where God meets you.*

Some days, the flow feels strong. Other days, it feels quiet. But the source remains.

And as you stay connected, the flow continues.

There will be moments when life feels demanding again. Moments when you feel stretched. Moments when you are called to give more than you think you have. But here is the key insight that changes everything:

You are not giving from emptiness. You are giving from overflow. Because when your life is rooted in the deep, you are not just sustained—you are supplied in such a way that you can supply others.

This does not mean you will never feel tired. It does not mean you will never need to pause.

Even rivers have rhythms. But it does mean that you are no longer limited by what you can produce on your own. There is something greater at work within you. And that something is not meant to stay contained. It is meant to flow.

As you reflect on this journey—from source, to seed, to secret, to strength, to separation—you begin to see a pattern.

God was never just building a life that survives. He was forming a life that flows.

- ✓ *A life that carries something deeper.*
- ✓ *A life that remains steady in changing seasons.*
- ✓ *A life that becomes a point of reference for others.*

And so, the question that remains is not just about what you have received.
It is about how you will live.
Will you continue to depend only on what is around you?
Or will you step into a life where something within you is constantly flowing?
Because when you begin to live this way, something shifts—not only in you, but through you. You become a quiet strength in uncertain spaces.
A steady voice in anxious environments.
A source of life where there is need. Not because you are trying to be different. But because you are living from the deep.
And when you live from the deep, you do not just experience God's supply.
You become part of how He supplies the world around you. You become the flow.

Declaration:
I am not just sustained—I am a channel of God's supply.
Rivers of living water flow from within me.
I will carry life, strength, and hope to those around me.

BONUS CHAPTER
WHEN THE DEEP IS BLOCKED

Opening Quote:

"The absence of flow is not the absence of source—it is often the presence of a blockage."

There is a question that must be faced honestly, especially after everything you have journeyed through in this book:

If the deep is real…

If the source is within…

If the flow is available…

Then why do we sometimes still feel dry?

Why are there seasons when the flow seems restricted?

Why do we feel disconnected, drained, or distant, even though we know what is true?

The answer is not always that the source has stopped.

More often, it is that something has blocked the flow.

A river does not cease to exist because it is obstructed. It continues beneath, pressing, waiting, ready to move again the moment the blockage is removed. In the same way, the deep within you is not easily destroyed—but it can be hindered.

Not by God's absence, but by subtle shifts within us.

This chapter is not about condemnation. It is about clarity. Because once you recognize what blocks the flow, you can begin to restore it.

And restoration, in the hands of God, is always possible.

The Quiet Grip of Fear

Fear rarely announces itself loudly. It does not always appear as panic.

Sometimes, it comes as hesitation.

As overthinking.

As the quiet pull to withdraw.

At its core, fear is a shift in focus—from God's sufficiency to your limitations.

It causes you to question what you once trusted.

To hold back where you once moved forward.

To shrink where you were meant to stand.

Over time, fear restricts flow.

Because the deep requires trust.

We see this in the story of the Israelites in the wilderness. Though they had witnessed miracles—the parting of the sea, provision from heaven—their progress was repeatedly hindered by fear. At the edge of promise, they hesitated. What God had opened before them, they could not step into, because fear redefined their perception.

The flow was not absent. It was resisted.

In contrast, the New Testament reminds us in *2 Timothy 1:7* that God has not given us a spirit of fear, but of power, love, and a sound mind. Fear may come, but it is not your source.

When fear settles unchecked, it narrows your world. It limits your movement. It causes you to live cautiously, rather than confidently.

Rohan experienced this in a very personal way.

After facing a significant setback early in his career, he became hesitant to take risks. Opportunities would come, but he would second-guess himself. Even when he felt prompted to step forward, something within him held him back.

He was not inactive. But he was restricted.

It was only when he began to confront his fear—naming it, praying through it, choosing to act despite it—that something began to open again. The more he stepped forward, the more the fear loosened its hold.

And slowly, the flow returned.

Fear blocks the deep not because it is stronger than God, but because it redirects your trust. And where trust is redirected, flow is reduced.

The Subtle Weight of Sin

Sin is often misunderstood.

It is not just about outward actions.

It is about inward alignment.

It is anything that creates distance between you and God—anything that interrupts the connection from which the deep flows.

Sin does not always feel dramatic. Sometimes, it is gradual. A compromise here. A neglected conviction there. A quiet drift. And over time, what was once clear becomes clouded.

The sensitivity dulls.

The awareness fades.

The flow weakens.

David understood this deeply.

In *Psalm 51*, after his failure, he does not just ask for forgiveness. He asks for restoration. *"Restore to me the joy of Your salvation..."*

Notice what was lost—not salvation itself, but joy.

The flow had been affected. David had not lost God's presence, but he had lost his experience of it. There was a blockage.

And the restoration did not begin with effort. It began with honesty.

- ✓ *Confession.*
- ✓ *Repentance.*
- ✓ *Realignment.*

In the New Testament, *1 John 1:9* assures us that if we confess our sins, God is faithful to forgive and cleanse.

Not reluctantly. Not partially. But fully.

Sin blocks the deep not because God withdraws completely, but because it disrupts our openness to Him.

Anita's story reflects this quietly.

She had once felt deeply connected in her spiritual life. There was clarity, peace, and a sense of flow. But over time, small compromises entered—choices she knew were not aligned, but justified in the moment.

Nothing drastic changed outwardly. But inwardly, something shifted.

She felt distant. Disconnected. Dry.

At first, she tried to push through it. To compensate with more activity. But the flow did not return.

It was only when she paused and allowed herself to be honest—acknowledging what she had ignored—that restoration began. It was not dramatic.

But it was real.

Peace returned. Clarity followed. And the flow resumed.

Sin may block the deep—but repentance restores it.

The Pull of Distraction

Not everything that blocks the deep is wrong.

Some things are simply… distracting.

Life has a way of becoming full.

Responsibilities increase. Noise multiplies. Attention is divided. And slowly, without intention, what once held your focus begins to fade.

Distraction does not confront you. It occupies you.

It fills your time, your thoughts, your energy—until there is little room left for stillness, for reflection, for connection.

Jesus speaks to this in the story of Mary and Martha in *Luke 10:41–42*. Martha is busy, active, doing what seems necessary. But Jesus gently points out that she is distracted by many things, while Mary has chosen what is needed.

The issue was not activity. It was attention.

The deep requires space. Not necessarily long hours, but intentional moments.

Moments where you are not rushing, not reacting, not consuming—but simply present.

Arvind found this out the hard way.

His life had become increasingly busy. Work demands, family responsibilities, constant communication—it all added up. He was productive, efficient, and constantly moving.

But something felt off.

He was no longer centered. No longer steady. No longer connected in the way he once had been.

It was not because he had abandoned his faith. It was because he had crowded it out.

When he began to intentionally create small spaces—early mornings without distraction, short pauses during the day—he noticed a shift.

Nothing external changed immediately.

But internally, the noise reduced. Clarity returned. And with it, the flow.

Distraction blocks the deep not by opposing it, but by replacing it.

The Trap of Wrong Dependence

Perhaps the most subtle blockage of all is misplaced dependence.

It is possible to believe in God and still depend primarily on something else.

Dependence can quietly shift.

- ✓ *From God to systems.*
- ✓ *From faith to control.*
- ✓ *From trust to self-sufficiency.*

And when it does, the deep is no longer your primary source. It becomes secondary.

This is what God repeatedly addressed with His people.

They trusted Him in crisis, but leaned on other things in comfort.

They turned to Him when nothing else worked, but drifted when things stabilized.

In the New Testament, Jesus reminds His disciples in *John 15:5*, *"Apart from Me you can do nothing."*

Not little. Nothing!

This is not a statement of limitation, but of alignment.

True flow comes from connection. When that connection is replaced, even subtly, the flow diminishes.

Karthik experienced this in a quiet but revealing way.

As his career progressed, he became increasingly capable. His confidence grew. His decisions became sharper. Success followed.

Without realizing it, his dependence shifted.

He still believed. He still prayed. But his reliance had moved.

From God… to himself.
And over time, something began to feel different.
Less peace. More pressure. Less flow. More effort.
It was only when he recognized this shift—when he intentionally returned to a posture of dependence—that the balance was restored.
Not by abandoning responsibility, but by realigning trust.

Restoring the Flow

If something has been blocked, it can be unblocked.
Not by striving harder.
Not by forcing outcomes.
But by returning.

- ✓ *Returning to trust where fear has taken hold.*
- ✓ *Returning to honesty where sin has created distance.*
- ✓ *Returning to stillness where distraction has filled the space.*
- ✓ *Returning to dependence where self-sufficiency has taken over.*

Restoration is not complicated.
But it is intentional.
It begins with awareness.
It continues with alignment.
And it is sustained through consistency.
You do not have to recreate the source. You only need to reconnect to it.
Because the deep has not disappeared.
It is still there. Still present. Still ready to flow.
And perhaps that is where this chapter gently leaves you—not with pressure, but with an invitation.
To pause. To reflect.
To ask yourself honestly:
What might be blocking the flow in my life right now?

And more importantly…
Am I willing to remove it?
Because when the blockage is cleared, even slightly, something begins to move again.
Not forced.
Not artificial.
But natural.
Like a river finding its course.
And when it does, you will discover once again:
The deep was never gone. It was only waiting to flow.

Declaration:
Nothing will block the flow of God in my life.
I release fear, turn from distraction, and realign with God.
My life is open, aligned, and flowing again.

About the Author
'GERARD ASSEY'

Gerard Assey is a Graduate in Economics, a PGD in Management (HRD) and holds a Doctorate in Leadership. Gerard holds several International Qualifications in Sales, Debt Collection, Training & Teaching, and is a 'Fellow' of the prestigious 'Institute of Sales & Marketing Management'-UK, a Certified NLP Practitioner, a 'Certified Trainer', an 'Accredited Management Teacher-Behavioral Sciences', a 'Certified Competency Facilitator', a 'Certified Management Consultant'- (the International credentials of a professional management consultant, awarded in accordance with global standards of the ICMCI); and a Certification from the University of Michigan in 'Successful Negotiation: Essential Strategies and Skills'

He is also a Member of the 'National Association of Sales Professionals' backed with several years experience in varied industries, both in India and Overseas. He also holds an 'Etiquette Consultant' Certification from the USA (by Sue Fox, Author of Best Seller: 'Business Etiquette for Dummies'. She has trained some of the top celebrities' world over). He was also a recipient of a scholarship for extensive training in Japan on 'Corporate Management for India'.

Gerard Assey is 'Founder & Chief Corporate Trainer' of the Group: '**Citius, Altius, Fortius Unlimited**'- an organization that **celebrated 20 years of Glorious Service** in 2021, focusing on 3 Core Competencies:

People. Performance. Profit; in functional areas of Sales & Marketing, HR & Organizational Development, covering Recruitment, Training & Consultancy!

Having managed organizations with large Sales Forces in India & Overseas, his specialization cover extensive areas of Sales Training (All levels - Presentation, Negotiation, Key/ Strategic Accounts Management & Managerial Skills for all sectors), Bid Proposal/ Capture Planning/ Management Trainings, Retail Sales, Customer Service & Customer Retention Programs, Training for Prevention & Collection of Debt, Self & Personal Development Programs (Time Management, Teamwork & Team Building, Business Etiquette & Personal Grooming, Leadership & Managerial Skills, People Management Skills, Train-the-Trainer etc), including preparation of Custom-designed Business Manuals for Internal (HR, Induction, and Sales etc) & External use (Instruction, User Manuals).

Gerard has successfully conducted over 6520 Trainings & Workshops (as of April '26) all across India, Middle East, Africa, Europe & S.E. Asia. Besides public programs conducted regularly, both in India & Overseas, he has some of the top names as clients whom he services from Single Owners to large Public & Government undertakings, covering all sectors, for their in-house needs.

His website: www.CollectionSkills.com is the only one in this part of the world to be featured in the 'Collections & Credit Risk Magazine-USA' under 'Who's Who in Training' and ranks TOP, along with other websites listed below on most search engines.

Gerard is author of 228 Books already (Apr 2026), all the books being available on all online platforms and outlets as E-books and Paperbacks

A few of our business related books:

1. Bite-sized Bits on Commonsense Management
2. Heart to Heart on Life's Principles'
3. How to become a Successful Manager
4. The Sales Professionals' Master Workbook of S.Y.S.T.E.M.S
5. The Professional Business Email Etiquette Handbook & Guide
6. The Professional Business Video-Conferencing Etiquette Handbook & Guide
7. Professional Presentation Skills
8. Exceptional Customer Service
9. Professional Tele-Marketing Skills
10. Professional Debt Collection Skills
11. The G.R.E.A.T. Sales & Service Workbook
12. Sales Training Advantage for Results (*The Ultimate Sales Training Manual to enable you stand out as a S.T.A.R.*)
13. CEO Daily Planner & Organizer
14. The Sales Professionals' Master Daily Planner
15. The Professional Debt Collector's Master Daily Planner
16. My Daily Planner & Organizer
17. MY EMERGENCY INFORMATION RECORD (Family Emergency & Peace of Mind Planner)
18. The Ultimate Therapist & Counselors Planner and Organizer
19. Building an Ethical Workplace
20. Managing Relationships at Work
21. Managing Business Meetings Effectively
22. Effective Delegation Skills
23. Goal Setting for Success
24. B2B Selling by Email
25. Professional Business Etiquette & Grooming
26. Dining Etiquette & Table Manners
27. Effective Networking Skills
28. Grooming, Etiquette & Manners for Teens, Young Adults & Future Leaders
29. Inter-Personal Skills
30. Get Ready, Get Hired!
31. Selling in a Recession
32. Effective Receivables Management in an Economic Downturn!
33. Real Estate & Property Sales Training
34. Credit Sales & Accounts Receivable Management

35. Selling Skills for Real Estate & Property Advisors
36. Take G.R.E.A.T. C.A.R.E!
37. Spa, Salon & Health Club Selling Skills
38. Selling Travel, Holiday & MICE Services
39. Selling Skills for Spa's, Salons & Health Clubs
40. Retailing in Salons & Spas
41. Selling Holiday, Vacation, Tours & Packages
42. The Power of Sales Referrals
43. Selling Luxury
44. Technical Selling Skills
45. Financial Advisors Sales Training
46. Dealing with Burnout at Work Monopolize Your Markets
47. Selling to Affluent Customers
48. Growing up with Grace
49. Financial Selling Skills
50. *The Effective Manager's Guide: Key Skills to Thrive*
51. From Aspiring to Inspiring: A Guide for New Managers on the Rise
52. The Power of Focus
53. Selling with Integrity: Sell Like Jesus The Perfect Role Model!
54. 31 Habits of Champions: Your 31-Day Journey to Greatness
55. Rejecting Grasshopper Talk: From Grasshopper to Giant-Killer-*Defeating Giants Daily!*
56. Navigate the AI-Powered Future of Bid & Proposals: Up-Skill to Stay Relevant with Alternative Career Paths & Opportunities
57. Hiring Sales Winners
58. Present with Impact
59. Success Unlocked: *Breaking Free from Habits that Hold You Back*
60. Complaints to Cheers, Feedback to Gold: Mastering Complaints Management
61. Thriving Together: *Cultivating Diversity, Equity, and Inclusion*
62. Coaching Skills for Sales Managers
63. Soaring to Success in Business & Leadership: Swifter, Higher, Stronger!
64. From Classroom to Podium: A Student's Guide to Powerful Public Speaking & Presentation Skills
65. Developing Self-Discipline
66. The CEO's 31-Day Power Plan: Unlocking Success through Essential Traits

67. Credibility Matters
68. A Winning Attitude
69. Bid & Proposal Management Using AI
70. Sales Forecasting: A Practical & Proven Guide to Strategic Sales Forecasting
71. Elevate & Energize: *50 Dynamic & Fun Activities for Peak Workplace Morale*
72. 'Sales SOS! Sales on Fire! *30 Days to Conquer Chaos & the Nightmares of Success!'*
73. Mastering Sales Managerial Skills: *Building High-Performing Teams & Driving Exceptional Results*
74. Eagle-Eyed Leadership: Unleashing the Power of 31 Lessons from Eagles
75. The Ultimate Employee Training Guide: *Training Today, Leading Tomorrow*
76. Being More Accountable at Work
77. Creating a Culture of Continuous Improvement
78. Effective Questioning & Listening Skills
79. The Power of Value Selling
80. The Growth Mindset
81. Mastering Professional Help Desk Skills
82. The Power to Lead with Empathy
83. Being Prepared: The Key to Unlocking Success
84. Youthful Spark-Youth Energizers, Activities and Games-Igniting the Fun in Youth
85. Ignite your Motivation for Success
86. Elevate Your Executive Presence: *Your Roadmap to Executive Excellence*
87. Smart Decisions: *Mastering Problem Solving with Strategic Solutions for Business Success*
88. Strategic Planning: *Developing and Implementing Strategic Plans to Achieve Long-Term Business Goals*
89. The Power of Stay Interviews
90. Developing G.R.I.T.
91. Adaptability
92. Diagnosis- *A Key Skill for Leadership*
93. The Burnout-Proof Salesperson: *The Master Guide to Preventing Stress & Burnout-* Strategies for Thriving in Sales
94. Learning from Failure: *Keys to Success*
95. Customer Success Management
96. Overcoming the Killers of Motivation
97. The C-Suite Code: *Mastering Skills for Executive Excellence'*

98. Dealing with Difficult Customers
99. Unlocking Your Potential: Mastering the Top 20 Life Skills for a Brighter Future
100. Nurturing Tomorrow's Leaders: *Essential Soft Skills Every Child Must Learn*
101. Lively & Fun Party Games for Seniors & Elders
102. Role Playing for Sales Champions: From Practice to Performance
103. Fun and Exciting Party Games for Kids
104. Case Studies for Sales
105. Role-Playing for Unbeatable Customer Service
106. Case Studies in Customer Service
107. Case Studies in Winning Negotiations
108. Case Studies in Management & Leadership
109. Case Studies in Human Resources & Talent Management
110. CEO Success Blueprint: The Essential Toolkit for CEOs and C-Level Executives
111. The Salesperson's Self-Coaching Guide: *Master Your Own Self-Coaching Plan for Success*
112. Overcoming Procrastination: *Your Ultimate Guide to Stop Delaying and Start Living Your Best Life*
113. When True Colors Are Exposed: *The Journey to Unmasking Humanity*
114. Life-Changing Habits for Teens: Teen Success Blueprint for a Bright Future
115. Workplace Stress-Free: *Proven Strategies to Thrive at Work and Beyond*
116. Objection Overruled: *The Ultimate Guide to Turning 'No' into 'Yes'*
117. Building Strong Teams: *A Comprehensive Guide to Team Building*
118. Ethical & Moral Leadership in Business: *Eliminating Unethical Practices & Building a Culture of Trust & Integrity*
119. Rising Strong: Building Positive: High Self-Esteem for a Fulfilling Life-*A Practical Guide for Students, Employees, Leaders & Entrepreneurs*
120 The Cheerful Mindset: Cultivating a Joyful Outlook Everyday
121. Leading Through Crisis: Case Studies on Crisis Management
122. Selling Beyond the Algorithms
123. MAGEN CAPD- Dialysis Record Journal

124. The Human Side of Healing: *A Master Manual on Professionalism, Patient Experience & Compassionate Care-From Treatment to Trust For Doctors, Nurses & Healthcare Teams*

From the Ministry side, Gerard graduated in the very first batch of Charis Bible College-India & had for over 9 years served as a Part-time Faculty at Charis Bible College-Chennai (Andrew Wommack Ministries-Colorado, USA).
He also holds a Diploma in Worship (a subject closest to his heart) from the JSOW and is also a graduate of the Advanced Mentorship Program (AMP) and the Circle Of Ministerial Engagement (C.O.M.E.) of Prophet Jerome Fernando and a Spiritual Son of the Esteemed Prophet.
An accomplished author of several Secular & Christian Books, Gerard has been on the board of a few international organizations and boasts of being the SON of the MOST HIGH GOD: An ordinary guy following an extraordinary GOD!

...And some of his most recent Christian Books being:

1. A Bouquet of Praises for My KING
2. Christian Jokes for the Serious Religious' Folks!
3. Jesus Healed You!
4. Praise24Ever! (also in Tamil version)
5. The 5G Network of GOD
6. Building Faith over F.E.A.R- FACE EVERYTHING AND RISE with JESUS
7. Hebrew and Greek Praise and Worship Words
8. Godly Mothers' and Grandmothers' Bible Story time for Kids!
9. Miracles of Jesus in Pictures
10. Raise your Praise all 365 Days
11. Thanking GOD with an Attitude of Gratitude
12. Meditating on the Attributes of GOD
13. Puppet Scripts
14. Alcohol Ruins, JESUS Reforms, Renews & Restores!
15. Habakkuk 2:2 Christian Daily Journal, Planner & Organizer
16. ABC of GOD's Word for Handwriting Practice
17. Daily Bible Verse Handwriting Practice (Building Godly Character & Faith through Cursive Handwriting Practice!)
18. Guiding Light: Fun & Faith-Building Bible Activities for Children

19. Rejecting Grasshopper Talk: From Grasshopper to Giant-Killer-*Defeating Giants Daily!*
20. Teen Titans of Faith: *Building Courage, Determination & Christ-like-Esteem*
21. I AM Empowered: *Unleashing Divine Power with Positive Declarations*
22. Be A Solution Provider-*From Passion to Purpose: A Biblical Guide to Being the Answer to the World!*
23. Miracles of JESUS
24. Parables of Jesus for a Meaningful Life!
25. A Grateful Heart: Importance of Sharing Testimonies of GOD's Grace
26. Melodies of Worship to JESUS: 31 Songs of Praise & Worship From My Heart to HIS!
27. I AM SO BLESSED!
28. My Daily Cup of Energizer
29. 31 Leadership Lessons *from* Jesus- *The Supreme Leader*
30. Peace Amidst Storms: A Biblical Guide to Conquering S.T.R.E.S.S.
31. Rise Above: 20 Biblical Eagle Lessons for Life's Triumphs
32. Godly Goal Setting: *The FAITHFUL Blueprint for a Purpose-Driven Life*
33. The Profound Attributes of our Mighty GOD: Understanding the 10S's of the Almighty
34. Worship Now, Worship Forever: *A Journey from Earthly Praise to Eternal Glory*
35. Unceasing Praise & Worship: *365 Days to Worship the King*
36. The ROAR Within: *Living with Purpose and Authority through the Power of the Holy Spirit*
37. From Potential to Purpose: Unlocking and Multiplying Your Talents & Gifts for Kingdom Impact
38. Songs from the Heart: *Worshipping GOD in Your Own Tune & Melody*
39. Awakening Praise & Worship: Hebrew & Greek Words to Raise Your Praise
40. Sing a NEW Song to the LORD Everyday: *Daily Devotions of Praise & Worship to Lift Your Heart & Glorify HIS Name*
41. *The* A.R.O.M.A. of True Worship: *Creating Worship That Delights God*
42. Becoming A Kingdom Champion: *Embracing God's Call for a Life of Purpose & Victory*
43. The Busy Businessman's Daily Devotional: 366 Crisp Truths to Start Your Day Strong
44. The Teacher's Heart: *Daily Devotions for Educators*

45. Anchored! *A 31-Day Devotional for Students Facing Life's Challenges*
46. Suddenly! Unlocking Unorthodox Breakthroughs through Unusual Worship
47. Overcoming Adversity: *Lessons from the Bible for Modern Challenges*
48. LORD, Don't do it without me
49. Kingdom Leadership: *Biblical Principles for Modern Leaders*
50. Heartprints of God- *Growing God's Way:* Daily Devotions for Kids to Shine Bright
51. Send Judah First: Let your Praises Go up First to See the Mighty Move of GOD
52. DIVINE MOMENTS: *Recognizing, Embracing, Preparing, and Walking into Life-Changing Encounters with God*
53. Be a Builder in the Kingdom: *The C.E.M.E.N.T. Guide to Creating a Lasting Legacy*
54. Unshakable: *Pillars of Godly Womanhood* (Pillars of Faith That Changed History)
55. Lead Like a Shepherd: *14 Essential Traits for Pastoral Excellence*
56. The Worship Leader's Arsenal: *Powerful Exhortations to Ignite Thanksgiving, Praise & Worship*
57. Women of UnShakable Faith: *31-Day Devotional for Strength, Purpose & Influence*
58. Called to Teach: *A Complete 10-Week Training Guide for Impactful VBS Teachers*
59. Strumming for the KING: Cowboy Songs of Faith & Fire
60. The Ultimate Youth Camp Playbook: *50 Bible-Centered Indoor Games to Engage, Equip, and Empower Teens*
61. Glad in HIS Presence: *David's Revelation of GOD's Love & Mercy*
62. The Spirit Behind the Sound: *52 Devotionals for Worship Teams*
63. THE COWBOY'S COMPASS: *Riding the Trail of Faith with Grit & Grace*
64. Worship as My Weapon: *Living Victoriously through the Power of Praise*
65. A Worshipper Always Wins: *Living a Life of Victorious Worship*
66. Worship That Leads to the Throne: *Practical Strategies for Worship Leaders to Inspire Their Team & Usher People into God's Presence*

67. Worship as Warfare: *Conquering through the Sound of Surrender*
68. Watchmen on the Walls: *A 31-Day Devotional for Worship Teams*
69. KINGDOM BUSINESS: *52 Biblical Principles for GODLY Leadership & Wise Decisions*
70. From Evening to Morning: *Rediscovering GOD's Sacred Hours*
71. Waves of Glory: *Worship through Dance, Flags, Staff & Sound*
72. WORSHIP TEAM BUILDER: *Guiding Your Team from Formation to Fruitfulness*
73. The Worship Leader's Master Training Manual
74. Skits for the King: Children's Plays for Every Church Occasion
75. Unbreakable: Building Strong Marriages and Families God's Way *(From Vows to Victory)*
76. Songs for my King: *A 31-Day Journey of Praise*
77. Building Powerful Children: *Raising a Generation That Will Shape the Future for God*
78. Character Before Chords: *The Heart of the True Worshipper*
79. 365 Days Before His Throne: A Worshipper's Daily Declarations
80. Broken to Built: *How GOD Restores Lives, Heals Hearts & Uses Broken People for HIS Glory*
81. Fear Did Not Come from God: *Discerning the Source, Dismantling the Stronghold & Walking in Power, Love & a Sound Mind*
82. THE GOD OF BEGINNINGS: *Positioning Your Life for What God Is About to Start*
83. HEALED ALREADY: IT IS FINISHED! Receiving What the Cross Has Completed!
84. A.D.D.E.D. Y.E.A.R.S. When God Overrules the Clock, the Diagnosis, and the Final Word
85. HALLELUJAH -The Sound That Heaven Understands *(Building a Life of Pure Praise)*
86. Worship in the Marketplace, Worship Beyond the Walls: *(Turning Work into Worship)*
87. ALPHA & OMEGA: *Living Secure Between the Beginning and the End*
88. JOYFUL NOISE: When Sound Becomes a Spiritual

Statement (When Heaven Responds to the Sound of Faith)

89. F.A.V.O.R.: Five Dimensions of Divine Advantage
90. THE UNBROKEN LAMB: The B.O.N.E.S. of Divine Precision
91. YOU ARE A WEAPON: Unlocking the Power of Worship That Breaks Chains and Opens Heaven
92. M.A.G.N.I.F.Y. *Seeing God as He Truly Is—and Living Above Everything Else*
93. THE HEALING COVENANT: *God's Provision for Healing, Health, and Restoration of the Whole Body*
94. THE DEEP: *Unlocking the Hidden Supply of God Within You*

Besides regularly contributing to business & trade journals, including international ones such as the 'Creative Training Techniques' and the 'Sales News' of the U.S.A, He is also a member of several prestigious bodies & trade associations, having participated in many Conferences & Workshops in India & Overseas.

Prior to his last assignment of leading & managing a large MNC as head, Gerard had a 3-year stint in the Middle East as a Consultant with a leading British Consultancy Firm.

As the past 'Official Country Representative' for the International Business Award- 'THE STEVIES'-(the business world's own Oscar) for about 4 years- he ensured a few Indian companies that qualify for the same every year!

Gerard can be contacted at:
Email: training@Sales-Training.in,training@CollectionSkills.com
Websites:

www.Sales-Training.in
www.EtiquetteWorks.in
www.CollectionSkills.com
www.RetailSalesTraining.in
www.SalesTrainingIndia.com
www.ManualPreparation.com
www.TrainingWithPuppets.com
www.FirstContactAcademy.com
www.SalesAndMarketingRecruiter.com

www.ingramcontent.com/pod-product-compliance
Ingram Content Group UK Ltd.
Pitfield, Milton Keynes, MK11 3LW, UK
UKHW021341190726
13845UKWH00027B/668

9 788169 340168